Do Cats Eat Turtles?

PAGE PUBLISHING
Conneaut Lake, PA

First originally published by Page Publishing 2024

ISBN 979-8-88793-355-9 (pbk)
ISBN 979-8-88793-360-3 (digital)

Printed in the United States of America

Do Cats Eat Turtles?

CYNTHIA G. LONGINO

Day 1

Hi, my name is Cindee. While visiting my aunt Gail at her home, we watched from her office window a family of turtles sitting on the tree limb that had fallen into the pond in her backyard.

There was a big daddy turtle, a mommy turtle, and two baby turtles. The daddy turtle had his head out of his shell so he could get some sun on his face. The mommy turtle and the two baby turtles were asleep in their shells.

3

Day 2

The next day, I noticed a black cat sitting on the tree limb where the turtles had been sitting the day before.

The cat sat on the tree limb all day. The turtles did not come to the tree limb that day.

I asked, "Aunt Gail, do cats eat turtles?"

"No, I do not think so," she answered.

Day 3

A mommy deer and two baby deer came to the pond. They drank water from the pond. They chased each other around the pond. After a while, they left.

I still did not see the turtles.

Day 4

The cat came back to the pond and was sitting on the tree limb where the turtles had sat.

A red fox with a long tail that was white on the end of the tail walked around the pond, stopped, and looked at the cat. He turned and walked in the opposite direction. The cat never moved. The fox walked around the pond, looking at his reflection in the pond. Then the fox walked back to the tree limb. He stopped and looked at the cat. The cat never took her eyes off the fox. The cal got into the attack mode, and out of fear, the fox ran away. The cat sat back down on the tree limb.

I asked Aunt Gail, "Are you sure cats do not eat turtles?"
"I do not think so," she answered.

9

Day 5

It had not rained in several days. The water in the pond was getting low. The sun was very hot. No animals came to the pond.

Not even the turtles.

Day 6

Finally, it rained. After the rain, a beautiful rainbow appeared above the trees. Aunt Gail, said, "Let's go outside and look for the pot of gold that is said to be at the end of the rainbow."

We walked to the tree line, and we did not find the pot of gold.

A blue crane flew down in the pond. She walked around the inside of the pond. She put her beak in the water and brought up a fish. She ate the fish. She walked around looking for more fish. She did not find any more fish. She flew out of the pond and sat in the tree that overlooked the garden.

Aunt Gail said, "She has a nest in the tree for her babies."

Day 8

A black horse and a brown horse with white spots came to the pond. They were drinking water and eating grass. The owner of the horses came to Aunt Gail's front door to let her know they had gotten out of their fence and he had come to take them home.

17

Day 9

I decided to go outside and look for the turtles. I walked around the pond and looked into the pond to see if they were in the water. I looked around the tree limb where the turtles had sat. I did not see the turtles.

The cat was walking toward the pond.

I ran back inside the house.

The cat took a seat on the tree limb where the turtles had sat.

Day 10

While I was walking past the window in Aunt Gail's office, I saw the big daddy turtle sitting on the other half of the tree limb that had fallen into the pond. He had his head out of his shell, getting some sun on his face. The mommy and the two baby turtles were crawling out of the water. They sat next to the daddy turtle on the tree limb.

I said, "Aunt Gail, the black cat did not eat the turtles. They moved to the other end on the tree limb that had fallen into the pond."

About the Author

Cynthia G. Longino lives in Mississippi. She has been in business for thirty-five years, Mr. Holmes Investigations, as a public record researcher. She plays golf and enjoys reading and gardening.